Hidden
SABBATH
Truths

Hidden
SABBATH
Truths

STEPHEN BOHR

Remnant
Publications
Coldwater MI 49036
www.remnantpublications.com

Published by
Remnant Publications
649 East Chicago Road
Coldwater MI 49036
517-279-1304
www.remnantpublications.com

Edited by Cari Haus
Cover design by David Berthiaume
Text design by Greg Solie • AltamontGraphics.com

Library of Congress Cataloging-in-Publication Data

Bohr, Stephen, 1950-
  Hidden Sabbath truths / by Stephen Bohr.
     p. cm.
  ISBN 978-1-933291-26-0 (alk. paper)
  1. Sabbath. I. Title.
  BV125.B64 2008
  263'.1--dc22

                              2008014190

08 09 10 11 12 • 5 4 3 2 1

Contents

Foreword

For many years, I have enjoyed listening to the scholarly teaching and preaching of Pastor Stephen Bohr. When ever he teaches or preaches you can always expect to be Biblically fed. This book is no exception. His journey through the scripture establishing a firm foundation for the Seventh-day Sabbath is so typical of all his presentations.

This treatise helps the Biblical student see how God has given the Sabbath as a relational experience for those who enter the Sabbath hours with Him. God set in motion through out eternity a system involved in a day in which He Himself rested and enjoyed His work of creation. Those who worship God during these sacred hours receive the blessing of His presence. Pastor Bohr has captured the significance of this concept and the fact that our creator set us an example of Sabbath rest.

James Finn
Associate Pastor

Dedication

To my trusted friend and fellow laborer
Elder James Finn, for holding down
the fort while I speak and travel.

To my beloved wife, Aurora, for her patience
and long suffering while I do the Lord's work.

Introduction

*H*ave you ever learned something totally fresh and new, after you thought you already had a very good understanding of the topic at hand? It's an invigorating and exciting experience, especially when that "something new" has been hidden—at least from your eyes—for quite some time.

That's what happened to me with the topic of the **Sabbath**. I was raised in a Sabbath-keeping home. I went to parochial schools where the Sabbath was taught. My father was a minister in a Sabbath-keeping church for more than 41 years, and I pastored in a Sabbath-keeping denomination for over 35 years. So, after all those years of Sabbath-keeping, not to mention hearing and preaching sermons about the Sabbath, I didn't think there was anything really earthshaking about the Sabbath that I hadn't heard.

Part One

Serious Questions

I was perplexed by some serious questions, however, over the years. As I read the story of creation, I wondered:

- Why, if the Sabbath was so important, did God not give Adam and Eve a direct command to keep it holy in the Garden of Eden, and

- Why, in Genesis chapter 1, God mentions an "evening and a morning" for every day except the Sabbath?

You see, although the Bible tells us clearly that God rested on the Sabbath day, nowhere are we told that Adam and Eve rested on the seventh day. So I always wondered, over the years, why God didn't give Adam and Eve a direct command to keep the Sabbath if that was His plan for them.

Genesis also tells us that there was an "evening and a morning" for every single day in

11

the creation week except one. And the evening and the morning were the first day, second day, third day—and on it goes right up through the sixth day. But when we read about the seventh day, there is no reference to an evening and a morning.

So I had these two questions for many years—actually, until just a couple of years ago. I was studying the book of Genesis again, when suddenly (and I believe this was through the Holy Spirit and a study of the Scriptures), God revealed two things to me which I had never thought of before. These discoveries have been very meaningful to me, and they are what I would like to share in this book.

Who the Story of Creation Is *Really* About

The first thing I would like for you to notice is that God—not Adam or Eve—is the subject of the first six days of creation. More than 30 times in the first chapter of Genesis alone we find expressions such as "God created," "God said," "God saw," "God called," "God made," and "God blessed." By using this level of repetition, God has made it very clear that *He did everything* during those first six days. Man, on the other hand, did absolutely nothing.

Genesis 1:31, where the account of creation ends, really underlines the fact that God was the subject during the first six days of creation.

In the words of the Bible: "Then God saw everything that **He** had made, and indeed it was very good. So the evening and the morning were the sixth day" (Genesis 1:31). So we see that it was God who made everything, God who saw that the things He had made were good, and God who was at the center of creation. Everything there was to do during that week, God did.

And this fact is just as true for the seventh day as for the other six. God was at the very center of the seventh day of creation as well.

> "And on the seventh day **God** ended **His** work which **He** had done, and **He** rested on the seventh day from all **His** work which **He** had done. Then God blessed the seventh day and sanctified it, because in it **He** rested from all **His** work which God had created and made" (Genesis 2:2, 3 emphasis added).

Somehow I think the writer wants us to know that God did everything. That it was God who not only worked the six days, but rested on the seventh day.

The Hebrew word *shabath* is used twice in Genesis 2:2, 3, and that word means to cease or stop. In other words, *shabath* doesn't refer to *how* God rested on the seventh day. The focus is on the fact that He stopped, or ceased from His labors.

An example or analogy of this would be in a court of law. When the prosecution "rests its case," that means they are finished presenting their arguments. It is not talking about the quality of the rest. It simply says they have stopped, or ceased to present the case.

And so the word *shabath,* as used twice in Genesis 2:2, 3, simply means that God ceased, He stopped creating on the sixth day. And the emphasis is on the fact that He did cease, rather than on His manner or mode of resting. This idea is supported in *Vine's Expository Dictionary*, where we find the interesting statement that "the writer of Genesis 2 verse 3 is not stressing rest from work, but rather God's ceasing from His creative work since it was complete." So these verses are talking not about the quality of God's rest, but the fact that God ceased, stopped and suspended His work of creating.

How God Rested

This leads us right into another question, for it is important to know *how* God rested on the Sabbath. Obviously it was a day of rest. And even though the word *shabath* says that He ceased creating after six days, it would be interesting to understand more fully *how He rested* before the weekly cycle began again.

To shed a little more light on this subject, allow me to quote from a magnificent commentary of the Old Testament, which begins with the fall of Lucifer and follows the history of God's people up through the period of the Israelite monarchy:

> "God looked with satisfaction upon the work of His hands. All was perfect, worthy of its divine author, and He rested, not as one weary, but as well pleased with the fruits of His wisdom and goodness and the manifestations of His glory" (*Patriarchs and Prophets,* page 47).

In other words, God didn't rest because He was tired. He was well pleased with the work He had created. For God, the first Sabbath was a day of contemplation, as He looked with satisfaction at all the things He had made.

According to the Bible, the first Sabbath was a day of contemplation not only for God but also for the entire heavenly host. We can read about this in Job 38:4–7:

"Where were you when I laid the foundations of the earth? Tell Me, if you have understanding. Who determined its measurements? Surely you know! Or who stretched the line upon it? To what were its foundations fastened? Or who laid its cornerstone, When the morning stars sang together, And all the sons of God shouted for joy?"

Notice that after challenging Job to consider where he personally was—or should we say was *not*—when God created the world, God mentions that in that great day all the morning stars sang together, and all the sons of God shouted for joy. In other words, the entire heavenly host also celebrated the work of creation on the seventh day. Together with God, they contemplated and meditated upon the magnificent work that God had done.

In reading this and other passages, it becomes obvious that God didn't rest on the Sabbath because He was tired. Isaiah 40:28 is a biblical text that clarifies this point:

"Have you not known? Have you not heard? The everlasting God, the Lord, the Creator of the ends of the earth, neither faints nor is weary. His understanding is unsearchable."

This verse, which is clearly talking about creation, informs us that God doesn't faint or grow weary. So when He rested on the seventh day, it was not because He was tired. It must have been some other kind of rest, a rest when He could contemplate and meditate on the masterpiece of a world that had just come forth from His hands.

In Exodus 31:17, God said that the Sabbath is a sign between Him and the children of Israel forever. "For in six days the Lord made the heavens and the earth and on the seventh day He rested and was refreshed." (By the way, that word for rested is the word *shabath,* the same word that was used twice in Genesis 2).

At the end of this verse the Bible uses another Hebrew word, *naphash,* to tell us that God was refreshed on the Sabbath day. *Naphash* also means to take a breath.

Imagine a world-renowned artist who has just completed a one-of-a-kind, truly magnificent piece of art. When he gives the final stroke of paint to the canvas, he steps back with complete satisfaction and lets out a long, whispered, "Ahhh. It's beautiful!" The artist is very pleased. And that's how God was. He ceased from His work and took a deep breath. He let out a satisfied sigh because everything He had made was absolutely gorgeous and beautiful. And the Bible says He was refreshed.

And then we catch another nuance of the manner of God's rest on the seventh day by going to Exodus 20:11, the last portion of the fourth commandment of God's holy law: "for in six days the Lord made the heavens and the earth, the sea, and all that is in them, and **rested** the seventh day. Therefore the Lord blessed the Sabbath day and hallowed it."

By going to the original language in which the Old Testament is written, we can find some very interesting things about this verse that gives the fourth commandment of God's law. The word "rested" as it is used here in Exodus 20:11 is a different word from the *shabath*, or word for rested, used in Genesis 2:2, 3. It's not the same word; it's the Hebrew word *newach*, which basically means "the experience of rest" after work. Now, Moses wrote both Genesis and Exodus. In both accounts he says that God did three things with the Sabbath: He rested on it and blessed and sanctified it. Why does Moses use *shabath* in Genesis 2:2, 3 and *nuwach* in Exodus 20? The simple reason is that Moses wanted to underline in Genesis that God ceased while in Exodus he wanted to describe the quality of God's rest. You see, the word *newach* is referring to what happens while God *shabath*, or ceased.

What Does It Mean to Enjoy the Experience of Rest?

This leads us to yet another question, of course. What does the Bible mean when it says that God enjoyed "the experience of rest"?

Although the word *newach,* which denotes the experience of rest, is used many times in the Old Testament, I would like to refer specifically to a few. The first is found in 1 Chronicles 22:9, where we are told that God promised David a son: "Behold, a son shall be born to you, who shall be a man of rest [*nuwach*]; and I will give him rest [*newach*] from all his enemies all around. His name shall be Solomon, for I will give peace and quietness to Israel in his days." The word *newach* here is linked with the idea of peace, tranquility and stillness after all the enemies of Israel have been defeated.

The next example is from Proverbs 29:17: "Correct your son, and he will give you rest [*newach*]; Yes, he will give **delight** to your soul." In this verse the idea of rest is linked with delight. In Zephaniah 3:17 we are told how God will delight in His people when they dwell safely in their land: "The Lord your God in your midst, the Mighty One, will save; He will **rejoice** over you with **gladness**, He will quiet you [*newach: give you rest*] with His love, He will **rejoice** over you with **singing**." Once again *newach* is connected with rejoicing, gladness and singing.

The last example comes from the book of Esther 9:17, 18. This passage describes a time when God's people had been delivered from their enemies. Haman had wanted to destroy all the Jews, but Esther had interceded, and God's people were delivered. And it says in that verse that God's people had rest, or *newach*. It is using the same word as was used in Exodus 20:11. The book of Esther tells us that, on this occasion, not only did God's people have rest, but they also celebrated that day with feasting and gladness.

In other words, *newach* was an experience of feasting and gladness. They were resting from the destruction their enemies intended to execute on them. So the word *naphash* means that God took a deep breath after creation in the contemplation of His work, and the word *newach* means that He experienced rest, tranquility, joy and gladness. As we have already noticed in Job 38:7, all of heaven rejoiced when God created this planet. The stars of heaven and the sons of God rejoiced in the work that God had created. We find a description of this joy in the classic biography of Jesus Christ, *The Desire of Ages*, page 769: "When 'the heavens and the earth were finished, and all the host of them' (Genesis 2:1), the Creator and all heavenly beings rejoiced in contemplation of the glorious scene. 'The morning stars sang together, and all the sons of God shouted for joy' Job 38:7."

In other words, it was a joyous rest in meditation and contemplation of the great work that God had done. And God took the seventh day simply to step back and look at the work that He had done, to meditate on it, and enjoy it with gladness and feasting.

When Was the Sabbath Blessed?

Now we come to another important question: exactly when was the Sabbath sanctified and blessed? I used to think that God blessed and sanctified the Sabbath day as the seventh day was beginning. In other words, the Sabbath was about to start, and God made some sort of announcement that He would be **sanctifying** and blessing the day that was just beginning. But as I studied into it more, I discovered that God did not bless and **sanctify** the seventh day until the seventh day was ended.

The fact that God didn't bless and **sanctify** the Sabbath until the end of the seventh day is an extremely important detail in the study of the Sabbath, as we are about to see. It also explains why God didn't command Adam and Eve to keep the first Sabbath. The Bible records that God Himself kept the Sabbath, and the heavenly beings kept the Sabbath. Rejoicing with feasting and gladness, they took a deep breath and enjoyed what God had made. But on the first Sabbath, this was the experience of God and the experience of the heavenly host. When it comes to man, Genesis doesn't tell us that Adam and Eve were resting.

The reason for this—and the reason why God didn't tell Adam and Eve to rest—has to do with the fact that God didn't bless or make the Sabbath holy until it ended. He didn't bless that day until it came to an end.

In the words of well-known Christian author Ellen White, "**after** resting upon the seventh day, God sanctified it or set it apart as a day of rest for man" (*Patriarchs and Prophets*, page 47, emphasis supplied). Did you catch that? She is agreeing with Scripture when she says the sanctification of the Sabbath happened *after* God rested on that day. By the way, I've read dozens of books on the

Sabbath, and no one has ever caught what I'm sharing with you except Ellen White. And she not only caught that point, it is all over her writings.

So God sanctified the Sabbath, or set it apart as a day of rest for man, after He rested on that day.

In another of her books, Ellen White wrote, "**Because** He had rested upon the Sabbath, God blessed the seventh day and sanctified it. **He gave it to Adam as a day of rest**" (*The Desire of Ages*, page 281, emphasis added). In other words, He set it aside for a holy use, and gave it to Adam as a day of rest, as a memorial of the work of creation and also as a sign of God's great power and love. So why did God bless and sanctify the seventh day as the Sabbath? Because He had rested on that day. In other words, He rests the whole day, and then He blesses and sanctifies the Sabbath. Following is another statement she made, in *My Life Today*, page 259:

> "The Lord's Day mentioned by John was the Sabbath. The day on which Jehovah rested after the great work of creation, and which He blessed and sanctified because he had rested upon it."

Notice that once again she is saying that He blessed and sanctified it because He had rested. And once more she writes "God blessed and sanctified the seventh day because He rested upon it from all his wondrous work of creation" (*Testimonies to the Church*, volume 4, page 247). So the day wasn't even made holy until it was over.

Why God Waited to Bless the Sabbath

"But why would God wait to bless and sanctify the Sabbath until it was finished?" I can almost hear you asking. The answer to this question is very simple. It is the presence of God that makes something holy. Each minute of the Sabbath that passed, God was making that minute holy. Each second, minute and hour that passed, God was making holy by His presence. And it wasn't until the last second, the last minute, and the last hour had passed that they were actually holy. Because it was the presence of God in those minutes and seconds and hours that makes those minutes, seconds and hours holy. And it could only happen after God had been present during those time periods, at the end of the Sabbath.

The Bible corroborates what Ellen White says on this matter. Notice Genesis 2:3. When I read this, I couldn't see how, with all my study and experience with the Sabbath, I had missed it before. But it is so clear and simple. Genesis 2:3 says, "Then God blessed the seventh day and sanctified it, **because** in it He rested from all His work which God had created and made."

Is that not clear? It says that God blessed the Sabbath day and sanctified it **because** in it He rested from all His work. Notice also in Exodus 20:11, which is the last verse of the fourth commandment of God's holy law, that it says, "For in six days the Lord made the heavens and the earth, the sea, and all that is in them, and rested the seventh day. **Therefore**" (that is, because He rested on the seventh day) "the Lord blessed the Sabbath day and hallowed it."

Is it a biblical teaching, then, that God rested on the seventh day, and then He made it holy? It is very biblical. We find it in Genesis 2:3 and we find it in Exodus 20:11. It says very clearly therefore the Lord blessed the Sabbath day and hallowed it because He had rested upon that day.

Tremendous Implications for Us

In a few moments, we're going to find out why this has tremendous implications for us all. But first, let me ask if it is clear in your mind that the first week was God's week. Since it was God who worked six days and God who rested on the seventh day, would you not say it was **God's week**? The week was not man's at all, at least not at this point, and not this first week. God did give the week to man, but this first week belonged to God. And He worked six, then rested on the seventh day as Sabbath.

Now we know the reason why the seventh day had no evening and morning. God has been resting from His work of creation since creation week. In the words of the apostle Paul, "And yet His work has been finished since the creation of the world" (Hebrews 4:3, NIV).

Paul wrote this more than four thousand years after creation. So what was Paul saying? Since creation week, what has God been doing with regard to this world? He has been resting from His works of creation, has He not?

In the words of Ellen White, "as regards this world, God's work of creation is completed, for the works were finished from the foundation of the world. But His energy is still exerted in up-holding the objects of His creation" (*Patriarchs and Prophets*, page 115).

Although God ceased creating after creation week, He still upholds and sustains that which He created during creation week. Ellen White also writes, "Although the Lord ceased His work in creating, He is constantly employed in uphold-ing and using as His servants the things which He has made" (*General Conference Bulletin*, February 18, 1897).

So God is still resting from His work of cre-ation in this world, because God has created no more. For God, so to speak, the seventh day did not come to an end, because He is still resting from His works of creation.

When Will God "Break" His Rest?

This leads us to an interesting question: when will God break His rest? As we will see later in this book, God will break His rest when He once again creates the world in six days and rests the seventh day.

Don't misunderstand. We know that for man, the Sabbath has an evening and a morning, a beginning and an end. But this first week was God's week, God's experience. He worked six days, He rested the seventh, and He is still resting because He has created no more. And when He finally breaks that rest to create this world again, He will work six days and rest on the seventh, just as He did at the very beginning.

"But what do you do with John 5:17, 18?" some people invariable want to know. Jesus Himself said in that verse that His Father had been working until now, and that He was working.

That question always comes up, and the answer is that Jesus is not talking about the works of creation in that verse. The work being spoken of in that passage is the work of sustaining and upholding the universe, and the work of redemption.

Just before making this statement, Jesus had restored the legs of a man who was paralyzed—to what they should have been in the beginning. But when Jesus restored that man's ability to walk, He wasn't doing the work of a new creation. He was upholding and restoring that which was already created. And the work that He spoke of just after this miracle was not a new work of creation, for that had been finished from the foundation of the world. It was the work of redemption.

But while for God there was no evening and morning to the seventh day, because God is still resting from His work, there was and is an evening and a morning for us humans. We know this because God told us to work six days and rest the seventh on a weekly cycle basis, and on the seventh day, the sun still rises and sets.

We also know that God told us to keep the Sabbath "from even to even" (Leviticus 23:32). Once God gave the week to man, then the seventh day had an evening and a morning. But this first week was describing God's working, and God's rest. So no evening or morning is mentioned with regard to God, and as we will see, this fact is very, very important.

Now, whom did God create the week for? The first week was God's week, as we have mentioned. But God doesn't need a week. He was obviously molding the week to give it to man. That explains why Jesus said, "the Sabbath was made for man, and not man for the Sabbath" (Mark 2:27). The first week belonged to God, because He worked six days, rested the seventh, and is still resting because He has created no more since the end of that week. He marked off that week, however, to give it to man.

"Like the Sabbath, the week originated at creation, and it has been preserved, and brought down to us through Bible history. God Himself measured off the first week" (*Patriarchs and Prophets*, page 111).

So what did God do the first week? He measured it off. You can almost see Him using a tape measure—counting, "One, two, three, four, five, six ..." as He measured it off as a sample for successive weeks to the close of time.

"Like every other, it (the first week) consisted of seven literal days. Six days were employed in the work of creation. Upon the seventh, God rested and He **then** blessed this day and set it apart as a day of rest for man" (*Patriarchs and Prophets*, page 111, emphasis added).

Did you notice again that God rested, and then blessed this day and set it apart as a day of rest for man? Ellen White is not alone in making these types of statements. Henry Morris, a Bible scholar and staunch creationist, wrote that "the Lord Himself had worked six days, and rested on the seventh, setting thereby a permanent pattern for the benefit of mankind" (*Biblical Creationism*, page 62).

What did **God** establish during creation week? A permanent pattern. He worked six days, rested on the Sabbath, and continues resting because He's created no more. Then He takes this measured week and gives it to man, saying, "Now you work six, and rest on the seventh. Your rest will not be continual, however, or without interruption. After you rest on the seventh, you're going to work six again, then rest on the seventh again, in a continuous weekly cycle."

Ellen White makes a remarkable statement about the weekly cycle on page 281 of the book *The Desire of Ages*: "**Because** He had rested upon the Sabbath, God blessed the seventh day and sanctified it, setting it apart to a holy use, and giving it to Adam as a day of rest."

When did God give the day of rest to Adam? After the day ended—which means that God did not give Adam the Sabbath when the seventh day began. Now let me tell you very clearly the reason God did not command Adam and Eve to keep **that first** Sabbath. In order to keep the Sabbath in harmony with the fourth commandment, Adam and Eve needed to work six days first.

The commandment says, "Six days shall you labor and do all your work, but the seventh day is the Sabbath of the Lord your God."

How could they have rested that first Sabbath and kept the commandment, if they had not previously worked six days? This is why Adam and Eve were commanded by God to keep the second—rather than the first—Sabbath of human history.

Furthermore, how could Adam and Eve have been commanded by God to keep the Sabbath holy, if the **Sabbath** wasn't holy until it ended? Because the first Sabbath wasn't made holy until the end of the day, God couldn't have told Adam and Eve to "keep the Sabbath holy," because it wasn't yet holy. It was the presence of God in that day which made it holy.

Furthermore, God gave Adam and Eve an example of Sabbath observance, but He couldn't have asked them to follow His example until after He had first given that example.

Now we know why God didn't command Adam and Eve to keep **that first** Sabbath. He couldn't, because the Sabbath was not yet holy.

How **could** He tell them to "keep the Sabbath holy," if it wasn't holy until the day ended?

An Important Question

"This is all well and good," I can almost hear you saying, "but what did Adam and Eve do on the first Sabbath, if they weren't commanded to keep it?"

Let me answer that question by asking a question of my own. Which day of the week were Adam and Eve created on? You can read it in Genesis 1:26–28, and also verse 31:

> "Then God said, 'Let Us make man in Our image, according to Our likeness; let them have dominion over the fish of the sea, over the birds of the air, and over the cattle, over all the earth and over every living thing that creeps on the earth.' So God created man in His own image; in the image of God He created him; male and female He created them. Then God blessed them, and God said to them, 'Be fruitful and multiply; fill the earth and subdue it; have dominion over the fish of the sea, over the

birds of the air, and over every living thing
that moves on the earth ... Then God saw
everything that He had made, and indeed
it was very good. So the evening and the
morning were the sixth day."

So Adam and Eve were created on the sixth
day. This means they were present when God
rested on the seventh day. They didn't see God
create anything, but they were able to observe
God's rest. And they certainly did see how God
rested on that day. We can see that very clearly
when we read Exodus 20:8–10, which tells us
what Adam and Eve did on the Sabbath, the very
first Sabbath:

"Remember the Sabbath day, to keep it
holy. Six days you shall labor and do all
your work, but the seventh day is the
Sabbath of the Lord your God. In it you
shall do no work: you, nor your son, nor
your daughter, nor your male servant, nor
your female servant, nor your cattle, nor
your stranger who is within your gates."

In this passage, God was telling the children of Israel about the Sabbath. The fact that the law was given directly to the children of Israel, however, doesn't mean it was only for them.

Many Christians would agree that the Ten Commandments apply to all people—except for the fourth. Now that doesn't make much sense, because the Bible tells us that if you break one of God's ten commandments, you're breaking them all. They either stand together or fall together. And as the passage we just read above goes on, God tells us why He wants us to work six days and rest the seventh:

> "For in six days the Lord made the heavens and the earth, the sea, and all that is in them, and rested the seventh day. Therefore the Lord blessed the Sabbath day and hallowed it."

God is asking us to follow His example. He worked six days and rested one. Now He wants us to do that too—because of His example. **I think you would agree that what parents exemplify is far more powerful than what they command.**

This is the foundational reasoning for keeping the seventh day holy, as given to us by God.

Do you see what is happening here? God is saying, "you work six, and you *newach* (or experience rest) on the seventh." And He even tells us the reason behind the injunction: "Because, at the very beginning of the world, I worked six days and rested on the seventh, and I want you to follow my example."

It would be impossible to follow God's example, of course, unless He had led the way first. Allow me to illustrate what I mean. Have you ever heard of Lego blocks? You may not have, since kids don't want them anymore. They only want video games. But there was a time when children loved to put Lego blocks together. They would fit one piece into another to build things, and some of the things they built could be pretty complicated.

I never had Lego blocks myself, or bought them for my kids very much. But I have seen fathers sit down on the living room carpet with their little son, and they say to that little boy, "Son, come here. I'm going to show you how to do this."

So the father starts putting piece upon piece, while his son is watching. Then when the father is all done, he takes the pieces apart and says, "Now you do it."

That's exactly what we have at creation. God observed the Sabbath, and then said to Adam and Eve, "Did you see how I did that? Now you do the same. Keep the Sabbath as you saw me keep it."

"After resting upon the seventh day, God sanctified it and set it apart as a day of rest for man. Following the example of the creator, man was to rest upon this sacred day that as He should look upon the heavens and the earth that He might reflect (that means to meditate) upon God's great work of creation, and that as he should behold the evidences of God's wisdom and goodness his heart might be filled with love and reverence for His maker" (*Patriarchs and Prophets*, page 47).

And what did God do when He rested on that sacred day? It was a day of joy and resting, a day of contemplation of His magnificent work, His masterpiece. God, together with the heavenly host, totally enjoyed what He had made.

Does it sound like the Sabbath was really a curse? The way many Christians today talk, you would certainly think that it was.

"Oh, the Sabbath was for the Jews that was this burden that nobody could bear," they say. You know, when people talk like that they are really **insulting** God, because God made the Sabbath. God exemplified Sabbath observance. It was God who said, "I worked six, you saw me rest on the seventh, you saw how I did it." It was God who gave Adam and Eve a scenic tour of the beautiful new world on that very first Sabbath and said, "Now that this day has ended, I'm setting it apart. I've given you an example, now I'm giving you the week. So you can work six days, but next Sabbath, you keep it just like you saw me do."

The Sabbath Essential for Man

"God saw that a sabbath was essential for man even in paradise," wrote Ellen White (*Patriarchs and Prophets*, page 48). Let me ask you, if the Sabbath was needed by man in paradise, would it not be much more necessary for us today **in a world of sin**? Of course.

"He (man) needed to lay aside his own interests and pursuits for one day of the seven that he might more fully contemplate the works of God and meditate upon His power and goodness. He needed a

Sabbath to remind him more vividly of God, and to awaken gratitude, because all that he enjoyed and possessed came from the beneficent hand of the Creator" (*The Faith I Live By*, page 31).

Are you starting to comprehend the purpose of the Sabbath? Do you see why God established the Sabbath right at the very beginning? It was so man would remember Him. That's why the fourth commandment begins "remember the Sabbath day to keep it holy." And that's why, at the end of the commandment, it is as if God says, "The reason why I want you to remember the Sabbath day is because it reminds you of the great Creator of the heavens and the earth, His **awesome** greatness, His power, and His love towards you, in giving you everything without even asking for it."

"Sabbath of the Jews"?

Many Christians today speak disparagingly of the Sabbath, calling it the "Sabbath of the Jews." This does not coincide with Scripture, however. Whenever the Sabbath appears in Scripture, it is called "the Sabbath of the Lord your God." Not once is the Sabbath referred to as the Sabbath of the Jews. It is always "the Sabbath of the Lord your God."

In Isaiah 58, God even calls the Sabbath "my holy day." In that same passage He also admonishes us to take our feet away "from stepping on my holy day." How dare someone say that the Sabbath was for the Jews! If the Sabbath really belonged to the Jews, if it was "their Sabbath," they should have been the ones to rest on it first. But they didn't rest on it first. God did. And right behind Him in keeping the seventh day holy were Adam and Eve, the parents of not only the Jews, but of all mankind.

God calls the seventh day "the Sabbath of the Lord your God" because He rested on that day, and that day belongs to Him.

"Now I want you to respect my holy day," He says. "I want you to respect my Sabbath, because I rested every single minute of it. I made it holy. It's my day, and if you want to enter my rest, you have to enter my rest on my holy day."

Many Christians today say, "You Seventh-day Adventists keep the seventh day as your Sabbath. I keep the first day, Sunday, as the Sabbath."

But did you know it's absolutely impossible to keep Sunday as the Sabbath? Do you know the reason why? Genesis makes it clear. You cannot keep Sunday as the Sabbath, because Sunday is not the day God rested.

It's that simple. If you're going to enter God's rest, you have to enter His rest on the day in which He rested. He never rested on Sunday; therefore, you can't enter His rest on Sunday. God did not rest on Sunday. He rested the seventh day. And if we want to enter His rest, we have to enter His rest on the day that He rested.

Do you understand what I'm saying? As I studied my Bible and examined these things, I realized that I had found the answers to questions that had bothered me for so long about why God didn't command Adam and Eve to keep that first Sabbath in the Garden of Eden, and why Genesis doesn't record an "evening and a morning" on the seventh day.

I also realized that the first week was God's week. That God worked six days and rested on the seventh. That because of that, the seventh day is His holy day. It belongs to God. I also learned that for God there wasn't any evening and morning on the seventh day, because after finishing His work on the sixth and resting on the seventh, He has continued His rest from that time until now.

For us there has been an evening and morning, but not for God, because God is still resting from His work of creation. He has created no more with regard to this world.

I also discovered why God did not command Adam and Eve to keep the Sabbath in the Garden of Eden. God could not command Adam and Eve to keep the Sabbath holy before He made it holy. God could not tell Adam and Eve "keep the Sabbath and follow my example" unless God had first given the example. And Adam and Eve could not really keep their first Sabbath until they had worked six days first. You see, the commandment not only requires resting on the seventh day. It requires us to work six days first. And at the time of the first Sabbath, Adam and Eve had not worked six days.

Part of God's Overall Plan

As we look at the Sabbath at creation, we see that it's part of God's original plan for the human race. It's not something God gave as an afterthought to the Jews in the wilderness. It was part of God's original plan, before sin. He gave the week and the Sabbath to Adam and Eve before sin.

"But the Sabbath really pointed to redemption," some people say. "It was all about redemption, about Jesus dying on the cross." The fact is, however, that celebration of the plan of redemption is a secondary meaning of the Sabbath. It is an important meaning, as we will note as we proceed in this study. But the primary, pre-fall meaning of the Sabbath is that God gave it as a memorial, a day of rest to look backward—not forward.

The original purpose of the Sabbath was to look back at the magnificent Creator and the work He had done. God wanted us to remember and consider His generosity and goodness in giving Adam, Eve and all of their descendents the beautiful gift of life, together with a truly incredible world to live in.

Clearly, the Sabbath was part of God's original plan for the human race. It was not an afterthought. And as we are going to see in the second half of this book, the Sabbath will also be observed in the earth made new.

The Sabbath points us backward, and also points us forward, to when God is going to break His rest. Once again He is going to create a new heaven and a new earth. He is going to create it in six days. He is going to rest on the seventh day, giving us an example, and then He is going to say, "Now, you work six days, and rest on the seventh day, and you come and worship before me, all flesh come and worship before me, on the seventh day, in commemoration of the new creation." How marvelous is this gift of the Sabbath that God has given us!

Part Two

*A*s we have seen in the first part of our study, Exodus 20:8–11 teaches that the original purpose of the Sabbath was as a reminder, or commemoration, of God's work of creation.

"Remember the Sabbath day to keep it holy. Six days you shall labor and do all your work, but the seventh day is the Sabbath of the Lord your God. In it you shall do no work: you, nor your son, nor your daughter, nor your male servant, nor your female servant, nor your cattle, nor your stranger who is within your gates."

Basically, God is saying that we should work six days and rest the seventh. He also gives the reason for this injunction, which is that He created the world in six days and rested the seventh. God set an example for us right from the start—an example He wants us to follow.

When you stop to think about it, the Sabbath is really an ordinance of creation. It came into existence before sin. It was instituted before the

47

cross of Christ was needed. So the original intention, or meaning, of the Sabbath has to do with the fact that it was a sign of creation.

Everything changed, however, when sin came into the world. The Sabbath had a second, additional function. And, as we will discover later in this book, there is actually a third function of the Sabbath as well.

The Sabbath Takes on New Meaning

The Sabbath took on new meaning when sin entered the world. We can read about this in Deuteronomy 5:12–15. This passage is actually a repetition of the fourth commandment, with the addition of a new **motivation** clause, or reason for keeping the Sabbath.

In Exodus 20, the Sabbath is presented as a commemoration of creation. In Deuteronomy 5, the motivation for keeping the Sabbath is different. This is the second, or post-fall, reason for keeping the Sabbath.

"Observe the Sabbath day to keep it holy, as the Lord your God commanded you. Six days you shall labor and do all your work, but the seventh day is the Sabbath of the Lord your God. In it you shall do no work—you, nor your son, nor your daughter, nor your male servant, nor your female servant, nor your ox, nor your donkey, nor any of your cattle, nor your stranger who is within your gates, that your male servant and your female servant may rest as well as you."

Notice the motivation clause: "And remember that you were a slave in the land of Egypt, and the Lord your God brought you out from there by a mighty hand and by an outstretched arm; **therefore** the Lord your God commanded you to keep the Sabbath day."

As we can see, the reason for keeping the Sabbath in this passage is not creation. It is redemption. The sign of redemption from bondage was an annual feast instituted by God and celebrated by the Jews, known as the Passover. This sacred ceremony pointed forward to the liberation that would come through Jesus Christ.

Because the God who created is also the God who redeems, the fall of man brought about this second, or post-fall, reason for keeping the Sabbath. The Sabbath, then, is a sign of both creation and redemption—a sign not only of the Creator God, but of the Redeemer God as well.

49

A Sign of Redemption

In the first portion of this book we took a look at the Sabbath and what it meant to creation. We will now consider how the Sabbath relates to the topic of redemption. Let us begin by considering the words of Jesus in John 5:45, 46. In this passage, Jesus is speaking to the Jews of His day, saying, "Do not think that I shall accuse you to the Father; there is one who accuses you—Moses, in whom you trust. For if you believed Moses, you would believe Me; for he wrote about Me."

Jesus was saying to God's people of that day, "If you believe Moses and the writings of Moses you would believe in me, for Moses wrote about me." In other words, "I am the central meaning and content of the writings of Moses."

The knowledge that Moses was really writing about Jesus puts a whole new light on Deuteronomy 8:3. We now know that this verse was centered on Jesus, for Moses wrote about Jesus. In this passage, Moses talked about the manna, or bread from heaven, that God sent to the Children of Israel during their trip through the wilderness. Here we learn that God humbled Israel through their experience in the wilderness, by allowing them to be hungry, then feeding them with a food that neither they nor their fathers had ever heard of before, a food called manna.

Moses also tells us that the reason God gave Israel manna wasn't just to provide them with physical food. God's primary intention was much deeper than that. There was spiritual meaning in the manna, which pointed forward to Jesus Christ, a meaning that Moses recognized when he wrote: "God gave the manna so you would know that man does not live by bread alone, but by every word that proceeds from the mouth of the Lord."

God gave Israel manna, then, to teach them that man does not live by physical bread alone. Instead, man should live by every word that proceeds from the mouth of God. The manna really represented the word of God, and God gave Israel the manna to teach them that if they were to survive, they were to live by the word of God just as surely as they depended on the manna provided by God in the wilderness.

Spiritual Food in the Desert

We can learn more about this in 1 Corinthians 10:3, 4, which tells us that during Israel's trek through the wilderness, they all ate the same spiritual food and drank the same spiritual drink. Why was the food and drink so spiritual? Because they drank water from the spiritual rock that followed them, and that rock was Christ.

So we can see that the manna had a deeper intention, a deeper meaning, than just being physical food. The manna was spiritual food, a symbol that represented the word of God.

What Is the Real "Word of God"?

When you think of the "word of God" you might automatically think of the Bible, but there is a deeper meaning for this, too. We can find out what—or who—the Word really is in John 1:1: "In the beginning was the Word, and the Word was with God, and the Word was God."

Now, who is the Word? It is none other than Jesus Christ. John basically said so later on in that same chapter, when he wrote that the "Word was made flesh and dwelt among us." So John was definitely talking about Jesus when he wrote about the "Word."

Interestingly enough, we also see that Jesus was deeply involved in the creation of this world. "He was in the beginning with God. All things were made through Him, and without Him nothing was made that was made" (John 1:2, 3).

God gave the manna to teach Israel that they should not live by bread alone, but by every word that proceeds from the mouth of God, and that Word was, in essence, Jesus. Through the manna, God was trying to teach Israel that the only way they could subsist spiritually was to partake of Jesus! The word of God was symbolized by the manna, and that Word was Christ.

"I Am the Bread of Life"

In John 6:48–51, Jesus explicitly referred to the manna, implying that it was a spiritual symbol of Himself. He was speaking to a group of Jews when He said, "I am the bread of life. Your fathers ate the manna in the wilderness, and are dead. This is the bread which comes down from heaven, that one may eat of it and not die. I am the living bread which came down from heaven. If anyone eats of this bread, he will live forever; and the bread that I shall give is My flesh, which I shall give for the life of the world."

So who does the manna represent? Jesus. The manna is the word of God, the word of God is

Jesus, and the manna represents primarily His life—His flesh.

"But why is this important?" you may be wondering. We find the answer in Exodus 16:19, 20. As we turn to this passage, let us remember what would happen if the manna was picked up on Tuesday and saved until Wednesday—it bred worms and stank. This happened whenever it was picked up ahead of time, whether the day was Sunday, Monday, Tuesday, Wednesday, or Thursday.

However, when the manna was picked up on Friday and saved for Sabbath, it was as fresh as ever. We can read about this in Exodus 16:19, 20, where Moses instructed the people to "let no one leave any of it until morning." Some of the Israelites did not heed Moses, however. They left part of the manna until morning, and sure enough, it bred worms and stank. The Bible records that Moses was angry with the people for disobeying on this point.

In Exodus 16:23, 24, however, we find Moses speaking to the congregation, telling the people, "Tomorrow is a Sabbath rest, a holy Sabbath to the Lord. Bake what you will bake today, and boil what you will boil; and lay up for yourselves all that remains, to be kept until morning. So they laid it up till morning, as Moses commanded; and it did not stink, nor were there any worms in it." So when the manna was picked up on Friday and saved for the Sabbath, the manna was as fresh on Sabbath as it had been on Friday.

Now, what did God want to teach by this miracle that He performed? We know that the manna represented Jesus, or His flesh, which He was going to give for the world. Jesus Himself said so.

Fast Forward in Time

Now let's take a look at what happened a little less than 1,500 years later, in the week when Jesus died. The Bible calls Friday the preparation day. It was late on Friday, and Jesus, who was hanging on the cross of Calvary, was about to finish His work of redemption. He was about to finish providing the means by which men and women could be delivered from slavery to sin, just as Israel had been delivered from literal slavery to the Egyptians.

Have you ever noticed that what happened in the Old Testament was literal, but when the fulfillment took place in the New Testament, it was spiritual? In the Old Testament we have the literal manna, literal rock, literal water, literal taskmasters, literal passing through the Red Sea, and literal deliverance. And each of these things pointed forward to what would be spiritual realities in the future.

When God was done creating the world, the Bible tells us that He "finished His works which He had created and made." Similarly, when Jesus died on the cross, He said the words, "It is finished." In the first case, the work of creation was complete. In the second case, it was the work of redemption.

It was late on the sixth day of the week when Jesus finished His work of redemption. The sun was about to set. We can read about it in John 19:30. After being offered some sour wine, Jesus cried, "It is finished!" Then, bowing His head, He gave up His spirit.

Notice the sequence of days involved in this series of events. It is very important to get the order of the days in our minds, because it will help us understand why Sunday can't be the seventh day. Although it is common for people to say that Sunday is the seventh day, it is really impossible.

Sunday is the first day, the day that Jesus was resurrected on. Many people are confused on this issue, especially in Europe, where the calendars in many countries actually begin on Monday. If those calendars were correct, Sunday would be the seventh day. But that doesn't agree with Holy Scripture.

In Luke 23:54–56, we read that Joseph of Arimethea went to Pilate and asked for the body of Jesus. He took the body of Jesus down from the cross, wrapped it in linen, and laid it in a tomb hewn from rock, where no one had ever lain. Before the end of the day Jesus said, "It is finished." It was the preparation day, and the Sabbath was about to begin. The women who were helping observed the tomb and how His body was laid. Then they returned and prepared spices and fragrant oils. The Bible says they rested on Sunday according to the commandment—right? Wrong! It says they rested on the Sabbath according to the commandment.

So Jesus died very late on a Friday, when the day was almost ending and the Sabbath was about to start. And after the death of Jesus it was the Sabbath, which is the seventh day of the week.

We know this because in Luke 24:1 we are told that Jesus was resurrected very early on the first day of the week. On the seventh day, however, He was resting in the grave. Jesus spoke about His sacrifice in John 6:51, where Jesus said, "I am the living bread which came down from heaven. If anyone eats of this bread, he will live forever. And the bread that I shall give is My flesh, which I shall give for the life of the world."

We have already mentioned that the manna, which was picked up on Friday, did not breed worms or stink on the Sabbath. This brings us to an important point: when Jesus rested in the tomb on the Sabbath day, His flesh did not begin the process of decomposing. His body was as fresh on the Sabbath as it had been on Friday, when He died.

Notice the messianic prophecy in Psalm 16:8–10 (NIV): "I have set the Lord always before me, because He is at my right hand, I will not be shaken. Therefore my heart is glad and my tongue rejoices." Notice, "my body also will rest secure." (The Greek word for "body" here means flesh, so Jesus is saying that His flesh also will rest securely, or in hope).

Jesus' body could rest in hope because it was in the tomb on the Sabbath and, as the psalmist says in verse 10, "You will not abandon me to the grave, nor will you let your holy one see decay."

In other words, the Messiah would rest in the grave with hope, and His body was not going to see decay or corruption. The body of Jesus could not see decay because He was the living manna. When the manna was picked up on Friday, it was as fresh on Sabbath as it was on Friday. Jesus died on Friday and, like the manna, His body was as fresh on Sabbath as it was on Friday. It did not decompose or even begin to decompose.

We can read more about this in a sermon from the apostle Peter on the day of Pentecost as recorded in Acts 2:25–27. Once again I am reading from the New International Version, which translates the text correctly, except that the word "body" should be translated "flesh." "I saw the Lord always before me. Because he is at my right hand, I will not be shaken. Therefore my heart is glad and my tongue rejoices; my body also will live in hope, because you will not abandon me to the grave, nor will you let your Holy One see decay." When the Greek is translated correctly, this is saying, "My flesh will live in hope." The New King James Version says, "You will not leave my soul in hell." But the NIV translates verse 27 more correctly: "You will not abandon **me** to the **grave** nor will you let your holy one see decay."

A little later in that same passage (verse 31), Peter interprets what we have just read: "Seeing what was ahead he spoke of the resurrection of Christ that **He** was not abandoned to the **grave** nor did his body (flesh) see decay."

Have you ever heard the teaching that the crucifixion took place on Wednesday and Jesus was resurrected on Sabbath? This prophecy makes that impossible. Jesus could not have been crucified on a Wednesday and resurrected on Sabbath, and still fulfill this prophecy because the only day that manna fell and could be fresh on the next day was Friday. So Jesus had to die and have His body "picked up" on Friday—not Wednesday, Thursday or any other day. This prophecy shows that Jesus was going to die on a Friday, that His body would rest in hope, and that it would not see decay. In other words, like the manna picked up on Friday, it would not breed worms or stink.

Now, these facts do not mean that when the Israelites ate manna, or when we eat communion bread today, it is the physical flesh of Jesus. No, we need to understand that His flesh was simulated through these ceremonies. We are not eating real physical flesh, but rather consuming His word.

Jesus had to answer questions about this Himself. In John 6:63 the people were basically saying, "Oh, He is trying to make us cannibals. We don't want to eat His flesh. That's not only gross, but forbidden in the law of Moses."

But Jesus wasn't saying to eat His physical flesh. He was saying that we could—and should—assimilate His flesh **spiritually** by studying the Word. Jesus physically was composed of flesh, but the Word is Jesus in written form.

That is why Jesus said to the people, "It is the spirit who gives life, the flesh profits nothing." In other words, it won't do you any good to eat my physical flesh, but "**the words** that I speak unto you, they are spirit and they are life." So we can assimilate the flesh of Jesus by partaking of His word. The manna represented the physical flesh of Jesus, but the spiritual flesh is His word.

By the way, 1 Peter 1:23 speaks of the Word of God being incorruptible—just as His flesh or body was. "Having been born again, not of corruptible seed but of incorruptible, through the word of God which lives and abides forever."

We can understand from all this that the Sabbath points not only backward to creation, but forward to redemption, or what Jesus was going to do when He died on the cross. Towards the end of the sixth day, in both cases, He was going to say, "It is finished." God rested on the seventh day after creation, and on the seventh day, after the great act of redemption was complete, the body of Jesus rested—but not without hope—in the tomb.

When we compare Exodus 16 with John 6, we see that there was a beautiful messianic prophecy wrapped up in the manna, or "bread of life."

One More Dimension

Did you know that the Sabbath has another dimension as well? The Sabbath has a future significance, a significance that, like the one related to redemption, would never have come about if man hadn't sinned. Before sin, the purpose of the Sabbath was to commemorate creation. After sin, the Sabbath still commemorated creation—but it also took on the new and very important role of pointing forward to redemption.

The beautiful "third dimension" of the Sabbath is that it also points forward to the end of time, when God will create a new heaven and a new earth (another task that became necessary through the entrance of sin into this world).

We can read about this in Isaiah 66:22, 23:

> "'For as the new heaven and the new earth which I will make shall remain before me,' says the Lord, 'so shall your descendants and your name remain.'"

Without a doubt, this verse is talking about the new heaven and the new earth, and it goes on to say, "'That from one New Moon to another, and from one Sabbath to another, all flesh shall come to worship before Me,' says the Lord."

The new moon marks the beginning of each new month for the Hebrews. The months are lunar months, so the months are reckoned by the moon just as the days are reckoned by the sun.

This verse is basically saying, "From month to month, and from Sabbath to Sabbath, shall all flesh come to worship before me."

Notice that this verse doesn't say "from one Sunday to another." Also missing is any statement about "all Jews coming to worship before me." The Bible is very clear: from one Sabbath to another, and one month to another, all flesh (that means every living person) will come and worship before Him. So the Sabbath, which is not for the Jews alone (as some would imply), will be celebrated every week in the new earth.

Why Monthly Worship?

This verse quite naturally brings up a question about why we will all go to worship the Lord from "month to month" as well as from Sabbath to Sabbath. We know that we will be worshiping before His throne, because that is where (as the book of Revelation tells us) people go to bow before God—on the "sea of glass" before His throne. But why would we go every month?

We can find the answer to this in Revelation 22:1, 2. Revelation is really helpful in explaining the Old Testament. You cannot understand Revelation without going back to the Old Testament, and you can't really understand the Old Testament without studying Revelation. It works both ways, which is why people who say they are "New Testament Christians" are really studying with one hand tied behind their back, so to speak.

In any case, Revelation tells us, "He showed me a pure river of water of life, clear as crystal, proceeding from the throne of God and of the Lamb. In the middle of its street, and on either side of the river, was the tree of life, which bore twelve fruits, each tree yielding its fruit every month. The leaves of the tree were for the healing of the nations."

So why is it that we are going to go worship before the Lord every month? As it states in Revelation 22, we will go to eat fruit from the tree of life.

Did you know that, even in the kingdom of heaven, our immortality will be "conditional"? In other words, we will continue to live because we eat from God's tree. We will not be "inherently" immortal. Our immortality will be derived from God's tree, and we will have to go every month to eat from that tree if we want to live forever and ever.

Why Weekly Worship?

You may also be wondering why, in the new earth, everybody will go to worship God "from Sabbath to Sabbath." The answer to this question is made abundantly clear in Isaiah 66, where we are told that God is going to make "a new heaven and a new earth."

A re-creation, or creation of a new heaven and a new earth, will be necessary because the earth will be physically decimated at the time of the second coming of Christ. It will return to the condition it was at the very beginning of its history, before creation. In Genesis 1:2 we read that "the earth was without form and void and the planet was in darkness."

We can learn more about the condition of the earth at the second coming of Jesus from Jeremiah 4:23, where the prophet wrote, "I beheld the earth, and indeed it was without form, and void; and the heavens, they had no light."

Now, if this planet returns to the chaotic condition that existed before creation, God will have to make a new heaven and a new earth if they are ever going to exist. He will have to make them just as He did at the beginning, and in order to do this He is going to suspend the rest that He entered into after He first created this world.

The evening and the morning of the seventh day at the beginning of time never came for God, because after the seventh day He created no more with regard to this earth. But when the earth returns to the condition it was in before creation, God is going to break His rest and start creating again.

Now, if it took God six days to create this world the first time around, how many days do you think He will take the second time? I used to think that when God creates the new heavens and the new earth He would somehow just say, "Let there be a new heavens and a new earth," and everything would be done.

Isaiah 66 tells us differently, however. There we learn that from week to week, or Sabbath to Sabbath, we will worship before the Lord as a commemoration of the creation of the new heaven and the new earth.

Now, you can't keep the seventh day unless you have the first six. If there weren't six days before the seventh day, it wouldn't be the seventh! So if we are going to go from Sabbath to Sabbath to worship before the Lord, it must mean that there are six days before the Sabbath.

The Powers of Heaven are Shaken

Have you ever wondered why God will need to re-create the heavens? We can learn the answer to this in Matthew 24:29, where Jesus tells us that "Immediately after the tribulation of those days the sun will be darkened and the moon will not give its light, the stars will fall from heaven and the powers of the heaven will be shaken."

So what is going to happen to the sun, moon and stars? They are going to be thrown out of their orbits, because the powers of heaven will be shaken. In Genesis 1:16, the Bible tells us that when God first made the world, He created the sun to rule the day, the moon to rule the night, and He made the stars also.

So the sun and moon have ruled the heavens since the creation of this world. But when Jesus comes, the sun and the moon will be thrown right out of their orbits. They certainly won't be lighting the sky over the earth during the millennium, because the Bible tells us that during that time the earth will be covered with darkness.

The whole solar system is going to be thrown out of whack, so to speak. When Jesus re-creates the new heavens and the new earth, He is going to restore the sun, moon and stars to their places.

Now here is the marvelous thing: at the beginning when God made the heavens and the earth, Adam and Eve were not eyewitnesses to the great act of creation. God made everything else before He made Adam and Eve. Even when He created Eve, God put Adam to sleep. So Adam did not see the creation of Eve, and Eve did not see God create anything either. They had to take Jesus at His word, and believe, when He said, "I am the Creator," and, "I made everything." They had to believe it because He said it. In other words, they had to walk by faith, not by sight.

But the beautiful thing is, at the end of time it's going to be different. God's people will not only be alive during the great work of creation, they will get to see it for themselves. Can you imagine what that's going to be like—to see God remake the earth again? To watch as He organizes it like He did in the beginning, puts it in order and fills it with His glory?

On the first day, He will say, "Let there be light," and the light will appear. Then the next day He says, "Let there be the firmament." And during all this majestic work of creation, God's people are watching what He is doing. On the third day He says, "Let there be productive land. Let there be trees and plants and flowers, and let them grow all over the earth."

Then these beautiful trees, plants and flowers will appear. And God will say, "Let the sun, moon and stars occupy their places again." And He's going to set the heavens in order, organize the cosmos, and place the sun, the moon and the stars where they were before they were thrown out of their orbits during the second coming of Jesus.

On the fifth day God is going to say, "Let the sky be filled with birds and the waters with fish." All of these creatures will have died because of the plagues, but God will repopulate the earth with them once more. Then on the sixth day, He will say, "Let the earth produce living creatures." And He's going to create all the wonderful animals that we have come to love. The very idea of cats in heaven brings a smile to the face of my wife. But there will be dogs, pet rats (you might not like them very well, but some people do), and all kinds of animals filling the earth again. The world is going to be a gigantic zoo, and everything will be perfect. In that new world, animals will not kill other animals anymore.

Then Jesus is going to say, "I have made this whole world in six days. Now come, I am going to give you the scenic tour." Then He will show us everything He has made when He suspended His rest and started working again. And just as He did after the first creation, at the beginning of this world, God will step back. He will take a deep breath and rest. And God will enjoy the experience of rest and joy and gladness. The whole heaven and earth will be filled with singing as He enjoys the work of His hands.

Like a master artist, He will contemplate the beautiful things He has created. Then, at the end of the first Sabbath day after the creation of the new world, God will say to His people, "Now this day is holy. I rested on it. Therefore, from now on, you will come into my presence from Sabbath to Sabbath to commemorate the glorious work of re-creation."

In other words, the Sabbath has a prophetic dimension, a future dimension. It points forward to the time when God will create a new heaven and a new earth, and His people will be eyewitnesses to that.

Once again He will establish the Sabbath after creation, as a sign that He's the wonderful, generous and loving Creator.

Some people have disagreed with the idea that there will be monthly and weekly cycles in the new earth.

"Pastor, haven't you read Revelation 21:23?" they ask me.

To answer these questions, let's take a look at that verse, and take a look at it carefully. There God is telling us that the city—and notice that it says "the city"—had no **need** of a sun or the moon to shine on them, for the glory of God illuminates them, and the Lamb is the light.

Now, here is an illustration to think about. How many of you have seen a person with a flashlight trying to find their way around at high noon? If you shine your flashlight on the ground in the middle of a bright, sunny day, can you even see one ray on the sidewalk? No, the flashlight is shining, but the light of the sun is so bright, so brilliant, that it's actually like you don't even have a flashlight.

That's what's going to happen with the sun and moon in the New Jerusalem. The sun and the moon will have to step aside and allow God to shine in the Holy City. We can find out more about this in Isaiah 24:23, where the prophet tells us that the moon will be disgraced and the sun will be ashamed. It doesn't say they will disappear—just that they will be disgraced and ashamed.

How can this happen? The verse goes on to explain: "For the Lord of hosts will reign on Mount Zion and in Jerusalem and before his elders, gloriously."

Now let us read one more statement, and a truly powerful one, from the pen of Ellen White:

"The powers of heaven are the sun, moon and stars. They rule in the heavens. The powers of earth are them that rule on the earth. The powers of heaven will be shaken at the voice of God. Then the sun, moon and stars will be moved out of their places." That's what we were talking about a little bit ago—she says they will not pass away, but will be shaken by the voice of the Lord.

Now let me ask you a question. Do you think the devil loves the Sabbath? No, the devil hates the Sabbath. In fact, it is the devil that has led many Christians to hate the Sabbath and call it a Jewish institution or a yoke of bondage.

The fact is, however, that the Sabbath is not a yoke of bondage, and it is not a Jewish institution. Jesus did not create the world for the Jews only; He created it for the whole human race. He did not come to redeem the Jews only; He came to redeem the whole human race. And the new heavens and earth which He will create, which will soon be commemorated by the Sabbath, will be for the saved regardless of country or culture.

The devil hates the Sabbath because the Sabbath exalts Jesus as Creator and Redeemer of this world. He also hates the Sabbath because it points forward to the new earth, where we will go to worship Jesus from one Sabbath to the next, and from one new moon to another. It should be no surprise that the devil hates the Sabbath that points forward to Jesus, because the devil hates Jesus.

If you want to know how much the devil hates the Sabbath, all you have to do is look at the history of the Sabbath. From the moment God gave the Sabbath in the fourth commandment, the devil tempted Israel to trample on that Sabbath.

They worshiped the sun, they worshiped other gods, and, in the words of the Bible, "did their own pleasure" on God's holy day.

So God sent them into Babylonian captivity because they trampled the Sabbath, desecrated and disobeyed it. The devil is very sly, however, and managed to use even this to his advantage.

"God wants them to learn to keep the Sabbath," the devil said, "so I'm going to tell them that they need to establish a whole bunch of laws that will make it virtually impossible to break the Sabbath." So the Jews enacted a long list of burdensome laws, supposedly to protect the Sabbath from being desecrated, and also so they would not be taken captive again.

One of these laws said that if you had false teeth, you had to take them out of your mouth on the Sabbath because carrying them would be a burden. If you had a prosthetic leg, you had to take that off, because it was a burden on Sabbath. You couldn't look in a mirror and pull out a hair on Sabbath, because that, too, would be committing a sin. You couldn't jump over a river because you might fall in and get wet. Getting wet in and of itself would not be breaking the Sabbath, but wringing out your robe or garment would be.

Nowhere in the Bible do you find these rules and regulations. They were rabbinical rules, not biblical ones. In other words, the devil led Israel from trampling on the Sabbath to idolizing the Sabbath and making the Sabbath a means of salvation. The devil was also busily preparing a way for Christians of the early church to look at the seventh day and say, "That Sabbath—it's a yoke of bondage, a burdensome bunch of Jewish rules and regulations. Let's not keep the Sabbath because of that. Let's keep Sunday because it's a happy day, a day that honors the resurrection of Jesus, instead of that old Sabbath yoke of rules and regulations."

Do you understand what the devil is doing? He wanted Israel to establish a whole raft of laws under the guise of wanting to protect the Sabbath—laws that would actually turn it into a yoke of bondage. And He wants to lead Christians to reject the Sabbath, to think that the Sabbath of the Pharisees is the same as the Sabbath of the Lord.

It is up to us to see that the rabbinical Sabbath is not really the Sabbath, but a distortion of the

Sabbath. Jesus didn't come to break the Sabbath, He came to deliver the Sabbath from the truck-load of rules that made it a yoke of bondage.

Jesus would never have given this rule-ridden Sabbath as a blessing! He would not have made a day holy, and blessed it, that was virtually impossible to keep. The fact is Jesus came to deliver the Sabbath from the bondage that had been created.

You know, Bible prophecy tells us that there was a "little horn" in the period of the Middle Ages that actually thought it could change God's law.

And there is a church in the world today that says, "We are the ones who changed the day of worship from Sabbath to Sunday."

Let me ask you, who do you think would like to see a change of the Sabbath from the seventh day to Sunday? Do you think God would want such a change? The answer to that question has got to be no! Satan is the one who would want such a change, because the original Sabbath pointed to the God who established it, but the change in the Sabbath points to the person who changed it.

The question becomes, then, whose authority are you going to accept? Will you accept the authority of God, who established the seventh day as the Sabbath, or will you accept the authority of the power that established Sunday as the day of rest? The issue is not one day versus another; the issue is, whose authority do you accept—God's authority or man's?

I can say from my heart that the Sabbath has been a great blessing to me personally. I enjoy it, and it certainly isn't a burden. It reminds me of my great Creator, it reminds me of my great Redeemer, and it reminds me that soon we will be in the kingdom, the new heaven and the new earth, wherein righteousness dwells. How is it with you, friend? What does the Sabbath mean to you?

About Pastor Stephen Bohr

Pastor Bohr loves the Lord with all his heart. He is committed to working for Him with all his mind, soul and might. He has dedicated years to the study of the prophetic message of the Bible.

He is best known for his groundbreaking video series, "Cracking the Genesis Code." He is a regular presenter on the **3ABN** TV network.

Pastor Bohr teaches "Foundations of Seventh-day Adventist Theology" at the Amazing Facts College of Evangelism. Presently he serves as senior pastor of Fresno Central Seventh-day Adventist Church and also as speaker for **Secrets Unsealed**, an organization committed to the preservation, proclamation and proliferation of the present truth message of the Seventh-day Adventist Church.

Secrets Unsealed is a non-profit supporting ministry based out of Fresno, California. We are located at the Fresno Central Seventh-day Adventist Church. If you would like to visit us, visit our web site to get driving directions to our offices. If you would just like to write us, please use our mailing address.

Secrets Unsealed • 1-559-264-2300
PO Box 6545 Fresno, CA 93703-6545
E-mail: info@secretsunsealed.org
www.secretsunsealed.org

Check out our online catalog filled with great books, videos, CDs, articles, Bible study materials, and more! Be sure to sign up for our free newsletter.